Outdoor Visits

The Lives of Animals, Insects and Plants in Nature, Illustrated for Children in Storybook Style

By Edith M. Patch

and

Harrison E. Howe

Illustrated by George M. Richards

PANTIANOS
CLASSICS

Published by Pantianos Classics

ISBN-13: 978-1-78987-163-0

First published in 1932

Contents

A Letter to the Boys and Girls

Dear Boys and Girls:

In this book you will read how Nan and Don visited animals and plants that live outdoors.

The animals and plants in this book live in different parts of our country. Most of them live in the North and in the South, too. You can visit many of the same kinds.

There are many kinds of animals and plants that are not in this book. You can visit those, too.

There are two ways to use this book. One way is to see how many things you can find that are like those in the book. It will be fun to find the same kinds of birds and the same kinds of flowers.

The other way is to see how many things you can find that are different from those in the book. You will like to find animals and plants that Don and Nan did not go to visit.

So you can have a good time with the different visits, too.

When you visit people in their homes, you are not rude to them. You have good manners. When you visit plants and animals you should be kind to them, too. You should have outdoor good manners.

Boys and girls with good manners do not harm what they find outdoors. They leave most flowers growing and do not break their stems. They leave the birds as happy as they find them. They help keep all the outdoor places lovely.

We wish you many pleasant visits!

Your friends,

Edith M. Patch,
Harrison E. Howe.

Fall Visits

A Pleasant Game

In summer, Don and Nan played outdoors most of the time. In September they went to school.

"Outdoors was one of our homes in summer," said Nan. "We lived there almost every day."

"Now school is one of our homes," said Don.

"Yes," said Nan, "when we go outdoors, now, we go for visits. We call on little animals."

"We call on plants, too," said Don. "And each visit is a pleasant game."

Goldenrod Honey

Don liked yellow flowers. So he went to visit some goldenrod.

Many insects visited the flowers, too. Don watched them come and go.

He saw the big black and yellow bumblebees. He heard the happy humming sound they made with their wings.

The bumblebees had a good time when they visited goldenrod flowers. They found nectar there to drink. The nectar was like sweet water and the bumblebees came for it.

Honey bees came to the goldenrod to drink the sweet nectar, too.

Honey bees change nectar to honey. They make golden-rod honey every fall and keep some for winter. There are no flowers for them to visit in winter. When they are hungry, they eat some of their honey for food. Goldenrod honey is good for bees.

Don liked goldenrod honey, too. His mother gave him some to eat with bread.

His mother told him, "Golden- rod honey is darker than clover honey. Some people like it much better than any other kind."

A Round Goldenrod Gall

When Don went to visit goldenrod plants, he found a gall on a stem.

The gall was a part of the stem that had grown large and round. It was the home of a little insect.

The insect that lived in this gall was a baby fly. It was white. It had no wings or legs. A baby fly is called a maggot.

When the maggot was hungry it ate some of the inside part of the gall. The gall was its home and its food, too.

The maggot ate gall food and grew fat. Then it rested without food.

The young gall insect was quiet all winter. In the spring its six legs and two wings grew.

Then it was not a maggot any more. It was a grown fly with dark wings.

The grown fly could not eat the same kind of food the maggot did.

The gall was not a good home for a grown fly. So the fly came out and flew away.

There was a little round hole in the gall where the fly came out.

When the fly with the pretty dark wings was ready to lay her eggs, she went to some goldenrod stems. She put each egg in a good place on a green growing stem.

Then the goldenrod stem began to grow in a queer way. It grew like a big round ball around the egg.

There was a baby maggot in the egg. When the maggot hatched it was in a round gall. The gall was its good home and its food, too.

The Yellow Spider

A yellow spider lived among the flowers on a goldenrod plant.

Don went to visit her one day. He did not find her at first and he thought she was not at home.

The spider was about the same color as the goldenrod. She hid among the yellow flowers and did not move. She was hard to see while she was so quiet.

At last Don saw the yellow spider. Then he laughed and said, "How do you do, Mrs. Spider? I came to see you and I thought you were not at home."

After a time a fly came to visit the goldenrod. It was a pretty fly with yellow stripes on its body. The fly was hungry and came to eat some pollen and drink some nectar.

The fly did not see the spider but the spider saw the fly.

When the fly came near enough, the spider jumped and caught it.

Don jumped, too, when the spider did. He was surprised to see a quiet spider move so quickly.

The goldenrod plants had no flowers in the spring time. So this spider lived among other kinds of flowers then.

For a while the spider lived among white flowers. She was not a yellow spider then. She was white.

The spider could change her color so she would be the same color as her home. She could be white among white flowers and yellow among yellow flowers.

This spider was shaped somewhat like a crab and her name was Crab Spider. She had four long legs and four short legs. She could walk sidewise and backward more quickly than forward.

Don told Nan about his visit.

He said, "I saw a spider that looked like a little yellow crab."

Blue Chicory

Nan liked blue flowers and she often visited chicory plants.

Once she went to call on chicory in the afternoon. The flowers were not open then.

So she went about eight o'clock one Saturday morning. The flowers were open. They opened about five o'clock and stayed open until ten or twelve o'clock.

Nan told her uncle about visiting the chicory. "Uncle Tom," she said, "I went to see some chicory flowers in the morning. They were open and looked as lovely as blue daisies."

Uncle Tom said, "Different kinds of plants have different habits.

"Some flowers stay open day and night. Some open in the dark and stay open all night. Some open in the morning and close before the middle of the day."

"Once I went to see the chicory in the afternoon," said Nan, "and I was surprised. I could not find any open flowers."

Nan asked if chicory is a weed. "People call chicory a weed when it grows where they wish to have other plants," her uncle told her. But in many places people grow chicory in their gardens.

Sometimes people grow chicory in the dark. Sometimes they cover the plants with sand.

Then the leaves are white and tender. They have a bitter taste but they are good to eat.

Some people cook these tender white bitter leaves. Some people like to eat them raw.

Chicory plants have big thick roots. The roots live in the ground all winter.

These roots are often dried and used like coffee.

Some people like a drink that is part coffee and part chicory. But some people do not like to have any chicory in their coffee.

Uncle Tom told Nan how people use chicory leaves and roots.

Then he told her about chicory honey. He said, "Sometimes people grow many, many chicory plants for bees. Honey bees visit the flowers and drink the sweet nectar. Then they change the nectar to honey." Nan said, "Once I saw some bees drink nectar when I went to visit the chicory.

"I wish I might have some chicory honey to eat with bread and butter." One day Nan dug up a chicory root and took it to school.

Her teacher said, "You may put it in the school garden, if you like."

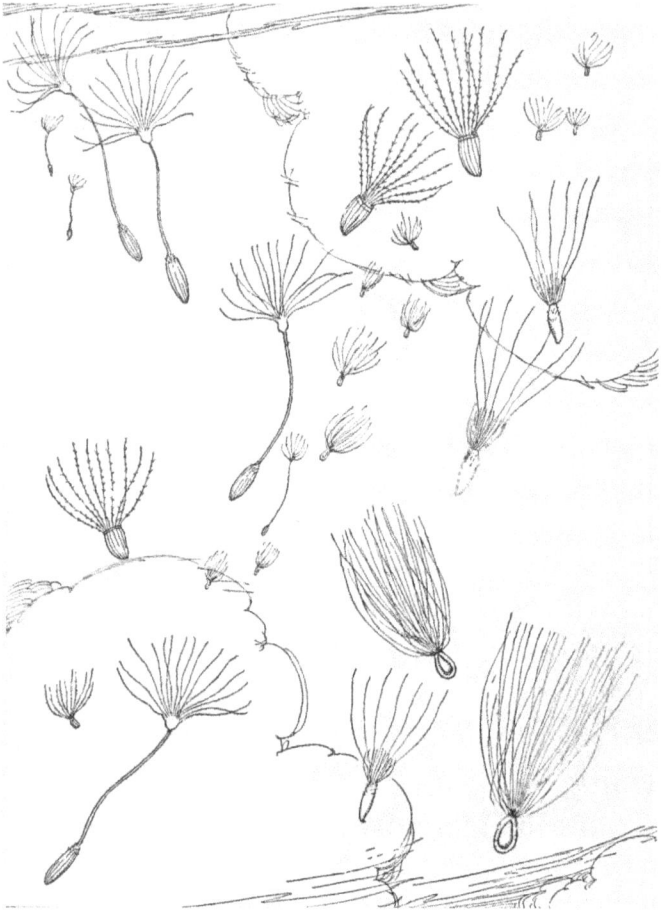

Flyaway Seeds

One fall day Nan said, "Don, shall we visit some plants with flyaway seeds?"

"Dandelions have flyaway seeds," said Don. "We played with some in the spring."

"They do not fly with wings as birds do," said Nan.

"No," said Don, "they go away where the wind takes them."

Nan said, "Uncle Tom told me that many plants have seeds that go up in the air like dandelion seeds."

"Perhaps," said Don, "we can find some to visit to-day."

Then Don and Nan went for a walk.

They found different kinds of plants with flyaway seeds.

They watched some of the seeds go away in the air.

When the wind went fast, the seeds went fast, too. Don and Nan ran but they could not catch the seeds.

"Each flyaway seed is a baby plant," said Nan. "It is going a long, long way from home."

"Perhaps it will come to a good place," said Don. "Perhaps the wind will stop and the seed will fall. Perhaps it will grow and live in a new home. Perhaps we can go to visit it then!"

Don and Nan liked the pretty flat milkweed seeds best of all the fly-away seeds.

The milkweed seeds were in a pod. There were many seeds in one big green pod.

Each milkweed seed had a brown coat. At one end of the coat were many fine white fibers.

The fibers were like soft hairs. They were as fine as the silk that a spider makes.

The milkweed pod opened when the seeds were ripe.

The sunshine and the dry air touched the seeds in the open pod. Then the fine fibers began to move.

The wind touched the soft fibers and they came out of the pod. The brown seed coats came with them.

A baby milkweed was inside each seed coat. So each baby milkweed had a ride.

The seeds went with the wind in the sunshine. They went high in the air when the wind took them up.

The wind went fast and took the milkweed seeds a long way.

The seeds fell to the ground when the air was still. They could grow in their new homes.

So there were many young milk- weeds a long way from their mother plant.

Don broke a leaf from a milkweed stem. Some juice ran out of the broken place. The juice was white.

He and Nan told Uncle Tom about their visits to the milkweed.

Uncle Tom said, "Some people call the plant milkweed because its juice is as white as milk.

"But some people have a different name for the same plant. They call it silkweed because the fibers on the seeds look like silk."

"I shall call it milkweed because its juice is white," said Don.

"I shall call it silkweed because its fibers look like line soft silk," said Nan.

Some Birds Go South

1. Swallows on the Wires

Don ran into the house and called, "Nan, come out and see the birds! They are all sitting on wires!"

So Nan went with Don to visit the birds. There were rows and rows of them.

Now and then a bird went away from a wire and hunted in the air. It found some insects and then it went back to the wire to rest.

"The brown-and-white birds are bank swallows," said Nan. "They make nests in holes in sand banks."

"Some of those birds are tree swallows," said Don. "They like to make nests in holes in trees. So people call them tree swallows.

"They have dark shiny backs that look green or blue. Their under feathers are white.

"Uncle Tom told me about them. He said different kinds of swallows often sit near one another on wires." "They seem to be waiting," said Nan. "I wonder why they wait." So they went to tell their uncle about visiting the birds.

"Why were bank swallows and tree swallows and some other swallows sitting on the wires?" asked Nan.

"Those wires are a good size for their feet," said Uncle Tom. "Swallows can perch on the small branches of trees and small stems of bushes. They can take hold of the wires with their feet, too, and so they like to sit there.

"They will soon go South, but they are in no hurry. They like to go in flocks. They fly by day. They stop to rest when they wish. And they hunt when they are hungry.

"Swallows go South for the winter. They find places where there is no snow. They stay where there are insects flying in the air."

"They have good times!" said Don.

2. New Coats for Bluebirds

One fall day Don and Nan visited the park.

They heard some birds. So they sat near a vine and were quiet.

Before long the birds flew to the vine. They found some dark berries on the vine and ate many of them.

They were bluebirds. They liked insects to eat but they liked berries very much, too. They had a happy time in the vine.

Don and Nan knew the bluebirds. They had watched the old birds go in and out of a box on a tree where they had a nest in the spring.

Father and Mother Bluebird did not look the same in the fall as they did in the spring. Their feathers were a little different.

The spring feathers dropped out and new feathers grew.

Father Bluebird had blue feathers with brown tips on his head and back. His breast was red. He had white under feathers near his legs.

The colors of Mother Bluebird were not so bright. Her head and back were gray.

When the young bluebirds first came out of the nest they had white spots on their backs and brown spots on their breasts.

Now the young bluebirds looked much like their father and mother. They were ready to go South for the winter with the old birds.

Uncle Tom told Don and Nan about the feather coats of bluebirds.

"In the fall some of their new feathers have brown tips," he said. "So their coats are not very bright.

"Before spring the brown tips will be rubbed off. Then the other colors of the feathers can show.

"That is why Father Bluebird looks so very blue in the spring."

"What a queer kind of coat!" said Don. "It is not so pretty when it is new as when it is old."

3. "Good-by Robins"

"Would you like to visit a robin roost?" asked Uncle Tom.

"I should, thank you," said Nan. "What is a robin roost?"

"I will take you and Don to one next Saturday," said Uncle Tom.

When Saturday came, Don and Nan went to the farm with their uncle. They had a pleasant ride in the country on the way to the farm.

After supper, Uncle Tom said, "Now we will go to the woods."

So they went to the woods where the trees were thick. They stood under a big tree and were quiet.

There were robins in the trees. They were sitting on the branches.

There were robins behind them. There were robins in front of them. There were robins over their heads.

And, on all sides of them, there were robins in the air flying to the trees.

Don asked his uncle about them.

Uncle Tom said, "Robins often come to trees at night. They like to roost on the branches. They like to roost near other robins.

"When they can find a good place, many robins go there to rest at night. Such a place is called a robin roost.

"At first only the father robins come to the roost in summer. The young robins come when they are old enough. The mother robins come, too, when their eggs are all hatched and their babies are all grown.

"Now it is fall and most of the robins near here come to this roost every night.

"They will go South before long. The next time you come to the farm there may be no robins here."

"Good-by, robins!" said Don. "I hope you will have a pleasant winter in the South."

"Good-by, robins!" said Nan. "Come back again next spring!"

Broad Leaves in Fall

A maple tree grew in the park. Its leaves were thin and flat and broad.

Snow would fall on the leaves if they stayed on the tree all winter. The snow would make the broad leaves very heavy.

The maple branches could not hold such heavy leaves. The branches would break if the leaves were too heavy with snow.

But the broad maple leaves did not stay on the tree in the winter. They fell to the ground in the fall.

The tree did not need leaves, then.

A tree grows in the spring and summer. While it is growing it needs to have leaves. Leaves help a growing tree to live.

Maple leaves are green all summer. They have strong fresh stems. The fresh stems do not drop from the branches.

In the fall a maple leaf changes its color. It is not green, then. It is red or yellow.

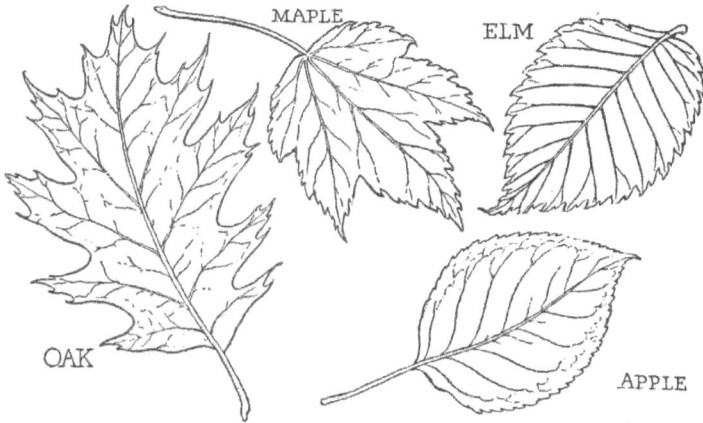

A maple leaf changes in other ways, too. The end of its stem is dry in the fall. The dry stem drops off the branch. So the old leaf falls to the ground when the tree does not need it.

Don and Nan went to visit the maple tree in the fall. They liked to play with the pretty leaves.

One day Nan said, "Leaves are falling from many other trees and bushes, too."

"Shall we pick up different kinds of broad leaves?" asked Don.

"Yes, that will be fun!" said Nan.

Fall Picnics

The bees were ready for winter. They saved good honey to eat.

The birds were ready for winter. Many kinds of birds went South. Some kinds of birds stayed near Don's home, but they could live in cold places in winter.

The trees and bushes were ready for winter. Most kinds of broad leaves were on the ground. Small brown leaf buds were on the branches. Green leaves would grow in spring.

Don thought about bees and birds and trees. Then he went to find his Uncle Tom.

"Uncle Tom," said Don, "what do animals with fur do? How do they get ready for winter?"

"Some of them have fall picnics," said his uncle.

"When I go to a picnic," said Don, "I have a pleasant time outdoors. And I have good things to eat."

"That is what the woodchucks do," said Uncle Tom. "But they grow very fat and go to sleep. They sleep in their holes in winter." "Nan and I like woodchucks," said Don. "May we go to their picnic?" "There are some woodchucks at the farm," said Uncle Tom. "We will go to visit them on Saturday."

Uncle Tom took Don and Nan to the farm and they found the woodchucks.

The woodchucks were lying on a stone wall. Their fur was gray and brown. The stones were gray and brown, too. It was hard to see the woodchucks.

Uncle Tom sat near the wall. Don and Nan sat there, too. They were all quiet.

After a long while the woodchucks came down from the wall. They ate some clover heads. There were seeds in the clover heads.

The woodchucks had a pleasant time eating their picnic dinner. The seeds were good food for them.

Nan and Don talked about fall picnics while they were going home from the farm.

"Uncle Tom, do other animals have picnics and grow fat?" asked Nan.

"Some other animals grow fat in the fall and sleep while the winter is cold," said Uncle Tom.

"Squirrels have picnics," said Don. "They eat many nuts in the fall. But they do not sleep all winter. They hide some nuts to eat when they are hungry."

"I shall go to a squirrel picnic in the park," said Nan.

"We can visit some of the tame gray squirrels there," said Don.

What Do You Remember?

1. Colors

The words that are left out are names of colors. Tell what color should be in each place.

1. A __ and __ bumblebee came to visit the __ golden-rod.

2. A __ maggot lived in the gall on a goldenrod stem.

3. The spider was __ while it lived among the golden-rod flowers.

4. The milkweed seed had a __ coat and __ fibers.

5. Father Bluebird had __ feathers on his breast.

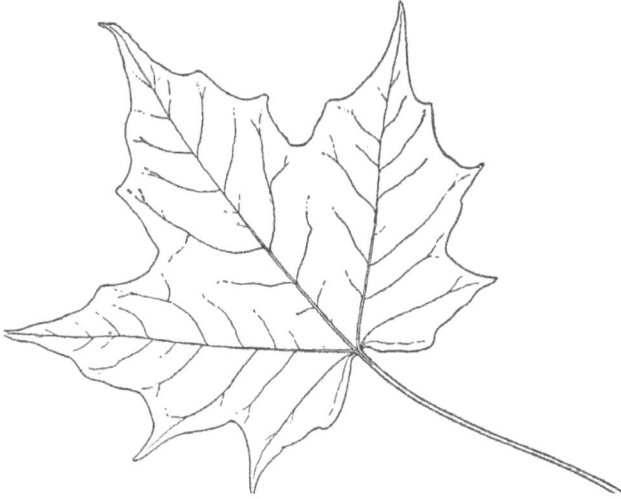

2. Leaf Pictures

Take two papers and make a picture of a maple leaf on each one.

In one picture put the color that the maple leaf has in summer.

In the other picture put the colors that the leaf has in the fall.

3. What Is It?

1. It has a fur coat.

It likes to eat clover heads.
It grows fat in the fall.
It sleeps almost all winter.
What is it?

2. It has a feather coat.
Its feet are very small.
It can perch on wires.
What is it?

3. It has a sweet taste.
It is made from nectar.
It is food for honey bees.
Boys and girls like it with bread.
What is it?

4. Can You Tell Which?

1. Did a little white maggot come out of the gall on the goldenrod, or did a grown fly come out?

2. Were the pretty blue chicory flowers open in the morning, or in the sunny afternoon?

3. Did the bluebirds and swallows and robins go North in the fall, or did they go South?

4. Was the silkweed plant the same as the milkweed plant, or was it a different kind of plant?

5. Was the bluebird nest on a branch of a tree like a robin nest, or was it in a box?

Winter Visits

Some Insects in Winter

1. Sleepy Bumblebees

One December day Don and Nan ran in the snow in the park. They talked about the trees and bushes.

They stopped to look at one bush and Nan said, "Do you remember this rose bush? It had lovely pink flowers in summer. The bumble- bees came here for pollen. We liked to hear their humming wings."

"We will ask our uncle about bumblebees in winter," said Don.

"In the late summer," said Uncle Tom, "the youngest Mother Bumble- bees go to flowers for nectar. They drink as much as they can. After a time they seem to feel sleepy.

"Then each very young Mother Bumblebee finds a good dry place and digs a hole in the ground.

"This small dry hole is her winter; sleeping room. She stays there alone until spring comes."

"I know what she does in spring," said Don. "She hunts for a good hole big enough for a summer home." "Yes," said Nan, "and then she makes bee bread of pollen and honey. And at last she begins to lay eggs."

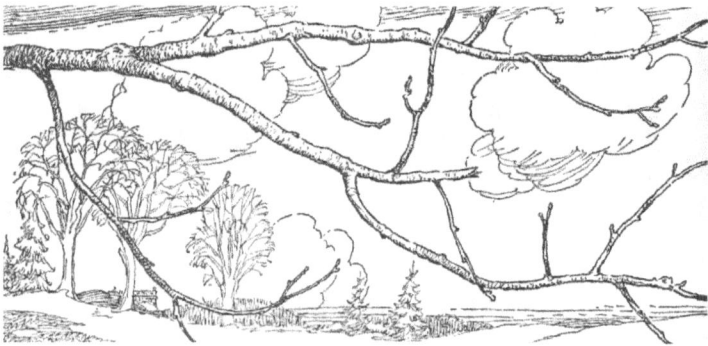

2. Eggs on a Branch

One sunny day Nan said, "Shall we call on the little wild cherry tree?"

"Yes," said Don, "and then we can see the branches. I wonder how they look with no leaves or flowers."

Don and Nan saw the slender brown branches of the wild cherry tree.

There was a mass of tiny eggs on a branch. The mass reached around the branch like a broad ring.

The eggs were covered with some shiny brown stuff. This kept the eggs dry. Rain or snow could not wet them.

Don said, "Here comes Mr. Gray. Perhaps he will know what it is."

Mr. Gray cut the egg mass off the cherry branch. He showed all the little eggs to Don and Nan.

He said, "There is a young caterpillar in each egg. If I let them stay on the tree they will hatch in the spring.

"So many caterpillars could eat all the leaves on this tree."

Don said, "May we help you take care of the trees? Shall we visit all the trees and find egg masses?" Mr. Gray said, "You may visit apple and cherry and plum trees and look for egg masses like these." So Don and Nan helped Mr. Gray take care of some of the park trees.

3. A Winter Butterfly

There was some water in the park on the ground. It was like a tiny pond with snow all around it.

The day was warm for December. So some of the snow had melted.

The sunshine touched one side of an old tree in the park. There was a hollow in that side of the tree.

A butterfly had been sleeping in the hollow. She rested all the cold winter days and nights. She did not feel cold while she was asleep.

On this warm day the butterfly waked. She moved her wings. She saw the bright sunshine outside and flew out of the dark hollow.

The butterfly was not thirsty while she was sleeping. But she felt thirsty, now. She had not had a drink for about eight weeks.

She liked sweet nectar to drink. In the fall she had found some in many flowers. But there were no flowers in the park in December. There was no nectar for her, now.

So what did the thirsty butterfly do? She flew down to the tiny pond of melted snow and drank some water.

Don and Nan were playing in the park. They saw the butterfly come down to the melted snow.

They were glad she found some water to drink. They did not scare her away. They liked to watch her.

"What pretty wings!" said Nan. "They are dark brown with yellow edges."

"Yes," said Don, "and there is black between the brown and yellow colors. And see that row of blue spots on the black!"

Mr. Gray was working in the park. Ted ran to tell him about the butterfly. He came to see it, too.

Mr. Gray said, "One name for this kind of butterfly is Yellow Edge.

"A Yellow Edge butterfly finds a dry hollow home in the fall. It sleeps there in cold winter weather. On warm days, like this, the Yellow Edge flies in the sunshine."

"I wonder what other kinds of butterflies do in winter," said Don.

"Will you tell us?" asked Nan.

"Different kinds of butterflies have different winter habits," Mr. Gray told them.

"Some kinds are eggs in winter. Caterpillars hatch from such eggs in the spring.

"Then each caterpillar grows and changes to a pupa. The pupa of a butterfly is called a chrysalid. When the butterfly inside the chrysalid i case is old enough, it breaks the case and flies away.

"Some kinds are caterpillars in winter. They go to sleep in the fall and do not waken until spring. They do not feel hungry while they sleep."

"Do any kinds of butterflies live all winter in their chrysalid cases?" asked Don.

"Yes," said Mr. Gray, "that is the way a Swallow-tail does. Then it changes to a grown butterfly in the spring."

Don and Nan ran home as fast as they could go to tell Uncle Tom.

"Mr. Gray told us how different kinds of butterflies live in winter," said Don.

"Do you remember what he told you?" asked Uncle Tom.

"He said some kinds are eggs in winter and hatch in the spring. Some kinds sleep until spring while they are young caterpillars. And other kinds change to chrysalids in the fall and wait until spring before; they change to grown butterflies. But Yellow Edges grow to be butterflies in the fall and find dry holes for winter homes.

A New Year's Party

1. "Chickadee Dee Dee"

One day Mother asked Don and Nan, "Would you like to have a party for some birds?"

"I think that would be jolly," said Nan. "Where may we have it?" "We are all going to the farm," said Mother. "You may have your bird party there."

"New Year's Day will come next week," said Don. "Shall we have our party for the birds then?"

"Yes," said Ann, "and then we can give them good things to eat and wish them a Happy New Year!"

When the children went to the farm, they tied some suet to a branch of a tree by the farm house. They took some nuts out of the shells and put them into cracks in the suet.

On New Year's Day a little bird came to the branch. Most of his feather coat was gray. But his throat was black and he had a black cap.

He perched on top of the suet and ate some of it. Then he clung with his head down and reached to get some from the underside.

Don and Nan laughed to see the little bird eat his treat with his feet up and his head down.

The bird put his bill into the suet and found a piece of nut.

He carried the nut in his bill to another tree. Then he put the nut on a branch and held it there with one foot while he ate it.

After he ate the nut he sat on the branch and sang, "Chickadee dee dee! Chickadee dee dee!"

While he was singing, some more little birds with black caps came.

They had very good bird manners. Only one bird came to the piece of suet at one time. They took turns.

Don and Nan said, "Happy New Year, Chickadees!"

And the little birds sang, "Chickadee dee dee! Chickadee dee!"

2. Suet Puddings for Woodpeckers

The next time Don and Nan went out to the tree the chickadees were not there.

Another kind of bird was eating suet. He had a warm black-and- white coat and some red feathers on the back of his head.

Don and Nan said, "Happy New -Year, Mr. Woodpecker!"

The woodpecker was happy but he did not sing. He had a good time with the suet.

His bill was big and strong. He tore off parts of the suet and pulled out some nuts.

The woodpecker pulled so hard that the suet fell off the branch.

Don and Nan ran into the house.

"Mother," said Nan, "the hungry woodpecker pulled the suet and it fell to the ground. What shall we give the birds for their party?"

"Would you like to make some suet puddings and put them into holes in the tree?" asked Mother. "I will show you how to make them."

So they warmed some suet on the back of the stove. They did not let it get too soft. They took it off the stove when they could shape it with their hands.

They put nuts with the suet. Then they shaped it into little puddings.

Don and Nan found some holes in an old tree. They filled these holes with little puddings.

"I do not think the woodpeckers can throw those to the ground," said Mother.

The woodpecker with the red on his head came for more suet.

His mate came, too. She had a warm black-and-white feather coat but she had no red feathers on her head.

Mr. and Mrs. Woodpecker had a happy time at the party. They could reach the suet and it did not fall to the ground.

After the woodpeckers went away, the chickadees came back to the party. They found the suet and nuts in the holes and ate some.

"I think that is a good way for them to have the suet," said Uncle Tom. "It will last many days."

3. Juncos

Don said, "Uncle Tom, will birds find fine seeds if we put them on the snow?"

Uncle Tom told him, "Some birds come to bare ground to look for food. If you put hay on the snow it will be dark and look somewhat like bare ground. Then you can put seeds near the hay."

So Don put out some seeds and hay.

After a while he and Nan looked out of the window and saw some juncos eating the seeds.

The juncos twittered in a very pleasant way while they ate.

These birds had dark gray backs and heads and throats and breasts. Most of their under feathers were white. Their tails were gray with white outer feathers.

"I am glad juncos came to our party, too!" said Nan.

Some Trees with Cones

1. White Pine

"Would you like to visit some trees with cones?" asked Uncle Tom.

"May we go this week while we are at the farm?" asked Don.

"Yes, you may go to-day," said his uncle.

"May we keep the different kinds of cones we find?" asked Nan.

Uncle Tom said, "When you learn the name of a cone tree and how its leaves grow, you may have some of its cones."

So they went to visit cone trees.

The biggest cones they found on a white pine tree. Some of these cones were about six inches long.

It took the white pine cones two summers to grow. So there were some small young cones on the tree and some that were big and old.

The short young cones were closed. They were not old enough to let their seeds fall out.

The long old cones were open. Their seeds fell out in September.

The white pine is an evergreen tree. It does not shed its old leaves until its new leaves grow. It is never without green leaves. So people call it "ever green."

The leaves are long and slender. They look somewhat like needles. So people call them "pine needles."

The leaves of the white pine grow in clusters. There are five leaves in each cluster.

Don and Nan counted the leaves in some of the clusters on a low branch.

They could not pick any cones from the pine tree. The cones were too high.

But they found some dry open cones on the ground under the tree. So they took them to show to their uncle. They asked him the name of the tree.

"If you will tell me how the leaves grow, I will tell you the name of the tree," he said.

"The leaves grow in clusters," said Nan.

"There are five long slender leaves in each cluster," said Don.

"The name of the tree is White Pine," said Uncle Tom, "and you may have the cones to keep."

"Does any tree have bigger cones than the white pine?" asked Don.

"Yes," said Uncle Tom. "Some other kinds of pines have much bigger cones.

"They grow where winter is not so cold as it is here."

2. Balsam Fir

Don and Nan went to visit another kind of cone tree. It was an ever- green, too.

The leaves were narrow and short. Some were a little longer than an inch. Some were about half an inch long.

They were green on top and they had two white lines on the under side.

There were some places in the bark that looked like blisters.

Don broke the bark at one of these places. Some balsam ran out. The balsam was a clear sticky juice and it had a pleasant smell.

Don climbed the tree to look for some cones. He did not find all of any cone. He found only the slender, middle part of each cone. He and Nan took these parts to the farm house to show to their uncle.

Nan said, "They look like little sticks standing on top of the branch. They do not hang down like our pine cones."

"The name of that evergreen tree is Balsam Fir," said Uncle Tom. "You can find the fir cones that stand up on the branches in summer. They are sticky then, when they are fresh and growing.

"Some of the cones on fir trees grow about three inches long. Some are longer and some are shorter." "Why do they look like pieces of broken cones now?" asked Don.

"The small outer parts drop to the ground in the fall," said his uncle.

3. Tamarack

"Come and look at all these little brown cones, Nan," said Don. "They are growing on a tree with no leaves on its branches in the winter time."

The cones were less than an inch long. They were all open. There were no seeds left in them.

Don and Nan picked some cones and ran to the farm house.

Uncle Tom looked at the cones and asked, "Can you tell me how the leaves grow on this kind of tree?"

Don laughed and said, "The tree has no leaves at all in winter. So I do not know how they grow."

"It has cones but it is not an evergreen tree," said Nan.

"One name for the tree is Larch and another is Tamarack," Uncle Tom told them.

Tamarack leaves grow in clusters. There are many fine short leaves in each cluster. They are green in summer. They turn yellow in the fall and then drop to the ground.

The cones are red in summer and brown in the fall.

Tracks on the Snow

Don looked out of the window at the deep snow.

"Nan," he said, "we can have an outdoor visit on snow-shoes."

"That will be jolly!" said Nan. So Don and Nan put on their snow-shoes and walked on the snow.

"If we play hide-and-seek we can find each other by the tracks," said Don.

"Perhaps we can find some animal tracks on the snow," said Nan. "Then we can follow them."

"I hope we may find tracks that have different shapes," said Don.

A dog ran across the snow. He ran under some trees.

Don and Nan saw him run but they could not see how far he went.

So they found his tracks and walked after him.

"I can hear him bark," said Nan.

After Don and Nan followed the dog, they came to some other tracks.

"Those are queer tracks," said Nan. "How could an animal make them? There are four marks close together. Then there is a space and then four more marks."

"An animal could not make them if he walked or ran," said Don. "But I think he could hop and make tracks like those.

"Perhaps a rabbit made them. And perhaps the dog is hunting for the rabbit."

After a while Don and Nan found the dog. He was digging in the snow near a heap of branches.

"The rabbit hopped into a hole under the branches," said Don.

"Now he is safe," said Nan. "The dog can not dig far enough under the branches to catch him."

The dog wagged his tail. Then he said, "Woof!" and ran home.

"I hear birds that sound like juncos," said Don.

"Yes, that is the way the juncos twittered when they ate seeds at our party," said Nan.

Don and Nan found some juncos eating seeds under a birch tree.

After the juncos flew away Don and Nan looked at the birch seeds on the snow.

"There are so many seeds that the snow looks brown," said Don.

"I shall draw a picture to show their pretty shapes," said Nan.

There were some different tracks in the snow near the trees. A mouse with white feet had made them when he came for seeds.

"An animal with little paws ran here," said Don, "and dragged his tail in the snow."

"We can follow his tracks," said Nan, "and hunt for his hole."

What Do You Remember?

1. Name Three

1. Name three trees that have their seeds in cones.
2. Name three trees that do not have their seeds in cones.
3. Name three kinds of tracks that Don and Nan saw in the snow.
4. The Yellow Edge butterfly has four colors on its wings. Name three of them.
5. Name three birds that came to the New Year's party at the farm.
6. Name three birds that were in the South on New Year's Day.

2. Choose the Right Word

Here are six words and six places to put them. Choose the right word for each place.

suet   twittered   black
seeds   slender   larch

1. The juncos ___ while they ate under the birch tree.
2. The white pine is an evergreen with ___ leaves.
3. The woodpecker and the chickadee like to eat ___ in winter but the junco likes ___.
4. ___ is one name for tamarack.
5. The chickadees have ___ feather caps on their heads.

3. Cone Picture

How can you tell this is not a tamarack cone? What cone is it?

Make a picture of this kind of cone on paper. Put the right colors in the leaves and cone.

4. Do You Remember?

1. What kind of insect had yellow edges on its wings? Where did this insect sleep on cold winter days? What did it do when the snow melted?

2. Why did Mr. Gray cut the egg mass off the branch of the wild cherry tree in the park?

3. Why did Don put hay on the snow near the seeds for the birds?

4. What is the pupa of a butterfly called?

5. How many leaves does a white pine have in each cluster?

6. What did the juncos find on the snow under the birch trees?

Spring Visits

Sounds of Spring

1. The Call of Wild Geese

Uncle Tom went to the farm one Saturday in March. Don and Nan went with him.

"If you hear a strange sound coming down from the sky, please tell me about it," said Uncle Tom.

"Will it be a pleasant sound?" Nan asked.

"It is the call I like best to hear in spring," said her uncle.

"What will make it?" asked Don.

"If you hear it, I will tell you," said Uncle Tom.

When it was time to go to bed, Don said, "We did not hear any strange call to-day."

Uncle Tom said, "Perhaps you will hear it to-night."

Don went to sleep but in the night something woke him. He went to the window and looked out. A big moon was in the sky and he liked to watch it.

While he stood by the window he heard something calling. The sound was high over the house. He did not know what it was.

He ran to Uncle Tom's door and said, "I hear it! I hear it! Come to the window and listen, too."

They woke Nan so she could listen with them.

"That is the call of the wild geese," said Uncle Tom. "They have been in the South for the winter. Now |they are flying to the North."

"It is very cold," said Nan. "How do they know it is spring?" "They feel like flying when the time comes. That is all I can tell you about it," said Uncle Tom.

"No man knows why the wild geese come when they do. Some springs there is still snow on the ground when they come. Often the ice is not all melted in the lakes when they fly over."

"I like to hear them," said Nan. "I think each one calls to tell the other geese that he is coming, too."

The next morning Don and Nan went outdoors. After a while they saw something like a big V in the sky. One goose made the point of the V and the other geese flew in two lines like the sides of the letter.

The birds that flew in a flock shaped like a letter V were wild geese. Don and Nan could hear them call.

They ran to find Uncle Tom. He was standing on a little hill while he watched the geese fly over. He could see them fly far away.

"I wonder how they know the way to their summer homes," said Nan.

"I wonder how they fly South in the fall and North in the spring without any maps," said Don.

"I wonder, too" said Uncle Tom, "and no one can tell us!"

2. A Frog Chorus

"Father," said Don, "what sound do you like best to hear in spring?"

"A frog chorus in April!" said Father. "When the ice is melted in the ponds and frogs come there to sing, I am happy to hear them."

"It is April, now," said Don.

"May we visit the pond?" asked Nan. "Perhaps the frogs are there. I should like to hear a frog chorus." "I will go with you," said Father. Before they reached the pond, Father said, "I can hear them, now!" Don and Nan stood still to listen. Then Don said, "I wish we could see them while they sing."

Father said, "If we talk when we are near them, they will hear us and stop singing."

"Then we will not talk," said Nan. They went to the pond and sat on some big stones. When they were very quiet the frogs began to sing. First a few sang. Then many sang.

Some of the singers had green backs and some had brown backs. They all had dark brown spots and their name was Leopard Frog.

When they sang, their skin puffed out at each side near the ears.

Don and Nan listened to the frog chorus with Father. Then they all went home.

"Once I saw some toads sit in the pond and I heard them sing," said Don. "They did not look like these frogs. They puffed out their throats like little balloons."

"Some kinds of frogs puff their throats out at the middle," said Father, "somewhat as toads do."

3. A Bluebird's Song

"Mother," said Nan, "what sound do you like best to hear in spring:

"A bluebird's song," said Mother. "It is a sweet and gentle song. It belongs to spring time for spring is full of sweet and gentle things.

"Buds on bushes and trees open into leaves and flowers.

"There are fresh colors to see and pleasant scents to smell.

"The bluebird's song makes me think of what is new and sweet.

"And so I have a name for it. I like to call it my Song of Lovely Beginnings."

One cool spring morning Don and Nan walked in the park on the way to school.

They came to the tree with a bird box on it. It was a box that Uncle Tom gave to Don and Nan. Mr. Gray put it up in the park for them the spring before.

Now, a little bird was looking in at the hole in the box. She had a blue back. Her under feathers were dull red near her head and white near her legs.

Another little bird was sitting on a branch not far from the box. He had a blue back, too. A very, very bright blue back!

The bird on the branch sang to the bird at the box. His song was soft and gentle.

Nan and her brother felt happy while they listened.

Don whispered, "I think his song is about beginning a new nest."

Ladybird Flies Away

Ladybird was not really a bird. She was a little beetle.

The two pretty wing-covers on her back were red. There was a small black spot on each one. Her two thin wings did not show. They were under her red wing-covers.

She had been in the home of Don and Nan all winter. She came into their house in the fall and found a crack or some other place she liked. Then she went to sleep.

She did not need much room for she was not so long as a fourth of one inch.

Ladybird did no harm in the house. She did not eat any rugs or clothes. She did not like that kind of food.

There was no food in the house she did like. But she was too sleepy to eat. So she was all right so long as she had a good place to rest.

Ladybird woke one pleasant day in spring. She walked about the room on her six little black feet.

She saw the sunshine at the window. She lifted her two red wing-covers and spread her two thin wings. Then she flew to the light.

Mother and Nan saw the beetle on the window glass.

"See the red beetle with black spots on its back!" said Nan.

Mother said, "That is a two- spotted ladybird. She has been resting in the house all winter. Now she would like to be outdoors. She has had nothing to eat. Perhaps she is hungry."

Mother opened the window and said, "Fly away, little Ladybird!" Her wings were thin and small but she could fly away with them. She went as far as the park and found a rose bush.

Ladybird was hungry but she did not eat the rose bush. She did not like to eat any kind of plant.

Ladybird liked aphids to eat. So it was pleasant for her that there were some on the rose bush.

The aphids were little soft insects | with long sharp beaks. They put the ends of their beaks into the tender rose stems and sucked the I juice.

The rose bush needed its juice to grow with. So the aphids were not good for the bush.

Don and Nan came to visit Mr. Gray in the park. They found him looking at the rose bush.

Mr. Gray said, "I am very glad Ladybird has come. She will help me take care of the bush."

Broad Leaves in Spring

1. Red Oak and Live Oak

"Do you remember how we watched the broad leaves last fall?"

Don asked his sister.

"Yes," said Nan, "they changed from green to bright colors. And | they fell to the ground."

"Shall we visit the big Red Oak?" asked Don. "Mr. Gray told us there would be new oak leaves late in May."

So Don and Nan went to the park to see the oak tree.

They found some fresh young oak leaves that were about half grown.

There were two kinds of flowers on the oak.

The flowers of one kind were near the ends of the branches where new leaves were growing.

They had no pollen of their own. They could grow into acorns if some pollen came to them from other red oak flowers.

The other oak flowers were on long slender parts that hung down in clusters.

These flowers had much pollen. The wind moved the clusters and blew some of the pollen to the flowers that had no pollen.

Mr. Gray told Don and Nan about the two kinds of oak flowers.

He said, "The buds of the flowers and leaves were on the branches all winter. The snow did not harm the small winter buds."

"Are there any evergreen oak trees?" asked Don.

"There is an evergreen oak in the South," said Mr. Gray. "It grows in places too warm for heavy snows. Its name is Live Oak."

"How do the leaves of Live Oak trees look?" asked Nan.

Mr. Gray showed them a picture of Live Oak leaves. They did not look like the leaves of Red Oak.

2. Holly Trees and Holly Bushes

"Will you show us pictures of other evergreen trees with broad leaves?" asked Nan.

Mr. Gray showed them a picture of a holly tree.

He said, "Holly trees grow best in places where there is not often much snow. Some grow near the sea in the North. But most of them grow in the South.

"The dark shiny leaves stay on the tree all winter. There are lovely red berries that stay, too.

"People like to see green leaves and red berries in winter."

"I wish I might see a holly," said Nan.

"There are some hollies growing in this park," said Mr. Gray.

"Real holly trees?" asked Don.

"No, real holly bushes!" said Mr. Gray. "They are near the pond."

Mr. Gray went with Don and Nan to the pond. Some bushes were growing in low wet ground.

"These bushes are one kind of holly," said Mr. Gray. "One name for them is Winterberry. They have red berries that stay on in winter. Hungry birds come to eat them. The leaves turn black in the fall and drop to the ground."

Mr. Gray told them about an evergreen holly bush that grows near the sea.

"So some kinds of trees and bushes with broad leaves are evergreens and some kinds are not," said Don.

Young Frogs

Mother Leopard Frog laid dozens and hundreds and thousands of eggs.

Her eggs were all in one mass. The mass swelled in the water and then it looked like clear gelatin.

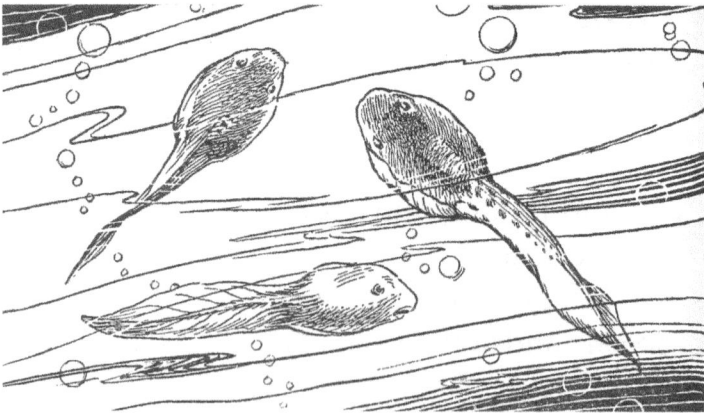

The eggs looked like little dark spots in the clear mass.

Mother Frog had a cold body and could not warm her eggs. The sun warmed them and the baby tadpoles hatched.

The tadpoles did not look like grown frogs. They had small mouths and large long flat tails.

At first the tadpoles had no legs. When they were old enough they had hind legs and after a while their front legs grew, too.

Don and Nan came to visit the tadpoles. They talked with Mr. Gray about them.

"Now, their mouths are large and their tails are small," said Nan.

Mr. Gray said, "Some time in the summer they will be changed to frogs. Then they will hunt in the grass.

"Some kinds of frogs stay in the water all summer. Leopard Frogs hunt for grasshoppers to eat.

"But every spring they live in the water for a while."
"And sing in a chorus!" said Don.

Don's Yellow Spring Flower

Nan said, "Don, last fall you visited goldenrod. What flower will you go to see this spring?"

"I shall try to visit a yellow flower, to-day," said Don.

Don went to the park to see his friend, Mr. Gray.

"Mr. Gray," he said, "have you any yellow spring flowers in the park?"

"We will go to the marsh and look," said Mr. Gray.

Don went with Mr. Gray to the marsh the other side of the pond. They found hundreds and hundreds of bright yellow flowers there.

The plants had their roots in the water. They held their stems up in the air.

The stems were hollow. Mr. Gray cut one stem to show Don.

"You may take this to Nan," said Mr. Gray. "We will leave all the others in the marsh. Then the place will be lovely for people to see."

Don looked at the sky and he looked at the marsh.

He said, "The sky is gray. There is no sunshine. But the marsh seems sunny."

"Yes," said Mr. Gray, "the sky is dull to-day but the marsh is bright with yellow flowers."

"These flowers have many names," said Mr. Gray. "But most people call them Marsh Marigolds.

"Buttercups and marsh marigolds belong to the same plant family."

White Feathers

Mr. and Mrs. Tree Swallow had dark shiny backs that looked blue or green in the sunshine. Their under feathers were white.

They came to the park and found a bird box. They saw a hole in the box and tried to go in.

Mr. and Mrs. Bluebird chased them away. The bluebirds had a nest in the box. So it was their own home.

Don and Nan saw the bluebirds chase the swallows. They told Uncle Tom about the birds.

Their uncle said, "Tree swallows like to make their nests in holes in trees. They like boxes, too.

"Tree swallows and bluebirds like the same kind of place for a nest."

"May we have a bird box for the swallows?" asked Nan.

Uncle Tom gave Don and Nan a good bird box. It was the right size and shape for tree swallows.

Mr. Gray put up the new box in a different part of the park. Don and Nan helped him choose the tree.

Mr. and Mrs. Tree Swallow found it. They went in and out of the hole. They both twittered with happy voices.

Mr. Gray gave Don and Nan some white hen feathers. He told them what to do with the feathers.

He said, "Tree swallows like white feathers for their nests.

"Put some of the feathers on the ground and bushes near you. Then stand still and watch the swallows." Mr. and Mrs. Tree Swallow saw the white feathers. They came and picked them up. They took them all into the bird box.

Then Mr. Gray said, "Nan, hold a feather in your hand as high as you can. Keep very quiet."

Don and Mr. Gray watched while Nan held the white feather.

Mrs. Tree Swallow flew near Nan's hand but she did not take the feather the first time.

Nan waited. She did not move.

The swallow came near Nan again. This time she took the feather out of Nan's hand and went into the bird box with it.

"Now, Don, you try it!" said Nan.

Don held a feather and one of the swallows came and got it.

Then Mr. Gray took some feathers and threw them up into the air. The wind blew them away.

The swallows flew after the feathers and caught some of them and took them into their box.

Nan's Blue Spring Flower

The side of a little hill in the park looked blue in May. It was covered with bluets.

The flowers were tiny. They grew close together.

Butterflies came to visit the bluets. They were thirsty and liked to drink nectar.

Little bees came to these flowers for nectar, too.

The insects put their mouths into the flowers to find the sweet juice.

Part of each bluet was shaped like a tiny tube. The nectar was in the lower end of the tube.

When a bee reached for the nectar she touched the pollen in the flower. Some of the pollen stuck to her long tongue.

So the bee took pollen from flower to flower.

There were two kinds of bluet flowers on the hill. Both kinds of flowers had pollen.

In the first kind of flower the pollen was high. It was near the top of the tube.

In the second kind of flower the pollen was low in the tube near the nectar.

The seeds in the first flowers could not grow with high pollen. They needed low pollen to make them live.

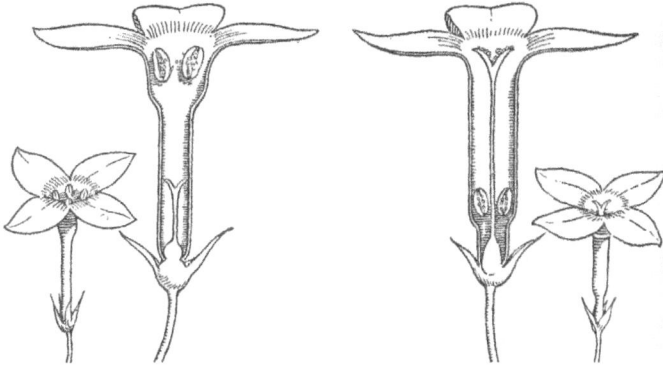

The seeds in the second flowers could not grow with low pollen. They needed the high pollen.

The baby bluet seeds could grow |because the little insects took the high pollen and low pollen to them.

Uncle Tom told Nan about the two kinds of bluet flowers.

Nan said, "I am glad the bluets give nectar to bees and butterflies. And I am glad the insects carry pollen from flower to flower. The insects and flowers help each other."

What Do You Remember?

1. Marsh Marigold Picture

Take a piece of paper and make a marsh marigold picture on it.

Use the right colors for the leaf and stem and flower.

2. What Did They Do in Spring?

Read a line under A. Find, under B, the right line to go with it.

A

1. The wild geese
2. Father Bluebird
3. Ladybird
4. The tree swallow
5. The frogs

B

took feathers to her nest,
had a chorus in the pond,
sang a lovely song,
flew to find some aphids,
called as they flew North.

3. Two Trees and One Bush

It is an evergreen.
It has red berries.

It has broad leaves.
It does not live in too cold places. What is it?
It is not an evergreen.
It has red berries.
It lives in a wet place.
What is it?
It is an evergreen.
It has acorns.
It has broad leaves.
It lives in the South.
What is it?

4. How?

1. How do bees and butterflies help bluets?
2. How do bluets help these insects?
3. When leopard frogs sing, how do their throats look?
4. When toads sing, how do their throats look?
5. How do aphids harm plants?
6. How do ladybird beetles help take care of plants?
7. How can a gentle wind help oak trees in spring?
8. How did the bluebirds keep one bird box for their own home?
9. How were the frog eggs warmed?

Summer Visits

Helping Mother Oriole

Mother Oriole wove her nest on a branch of an elm tree in the park. It was almost June before the nest was all ready for her eggs.

Father and Mother Oriole came to the park in May. They came from a place far away in the South.

Father Oriole came first. He sat on a high branch and sang.

When Mother Oriole came she heard the song. So she went near the tree where Father Oriole sat. They were glad to see each other.

Father Oriole was bright orange land black. There were some white feathers on his wings.

Mother Oriole had brown and gray and black feathers on her head and back. Most of her under feathers were a dull orange color.

Don and Nan heard the oriole in the park.

Mr. Gray told them, "Father Oriole whistles while Mother Oriole makes the nest. It hangs from a branch."

"How does she make a hanging kind of nest?" asked Nan.

"She weaves it with fibers," said Mr. Gray. "She hunts for strong stems of old brown grass. She takes fibers from stems of milkweeds and some other plants. If she finds a short string she is very happy.

"A long string is not good for her to use. If it is too long it may be caught around her neck or legs."

"I have some string," said Don. Mr. Gray cut Don's string into pieces ten or twelve inches long.

Nan put them on bushes near the elm tree.

Mother Oriole found the string and wove it into her nest.

After Mother Oriole wove her nest, she put a soft bed in it and laid her eggs.

When the young birds hatched they called for food. Then Father Oriole had no time to sit and sing. He helped Mother Oriole hunt for caterpillars for the baby birds.

In September all these Orioles started South. They had a long way to go to their winter home.

After the leaves fell from the elm tree, Don and Nan could see the hanging nest.

Nan said, "We helped Mother Oriole when she made that nest. We gave her short string for fibers."

A Stem with Three Sides

At first Don and Nan thought some plants in the marsh were grasses.

The leaves were shaped very much like grass leaves.

But they grew with their lower ends together in a stem that had three sides.

When the sun touched the leaves they looked very bright.

When the wind touched them their tips rubbed against one another. They made sounds like whispers.

Nan asked Uncle Tom, "What marsh plant has a stem with three sides?"

"Sedge!" said her uncle.

94

Some Very Small Snails

"I wish we had a little pet snail!" said Nan.

Uncle Tom told her, "There are snails in the marsh at the farm. I will take you to visit them."

Don and Nan went to the farm with Uncle Tom on Saturday.

"It is easy to find some snails in the day time," said Uncle Tom. "But these hide while it is light." "It will be fun to visit them at night!" said Don.

They found a snail moving on a sedge leaf.

"You may have it for a pet," said Uncle Tom, "if you will give it all the food it needs."

Nan put the snail into a glass that had a cover. Then she dug up a young sedge for it.

Don put some mud from the marsh into the glass.

Uncle Tom gave the snail some soft white leaves and stems and roots that he found under a wet stone in the marsh.

The snail laid some eggs on the mud. They were nearly round and they had no shells.

The baby snails lived in the eggs until they were three weeks old. Tiny shells grew on their backs before they came out of the eggs.

The young snails were so small no one could see them very well. They looked like moving specks.

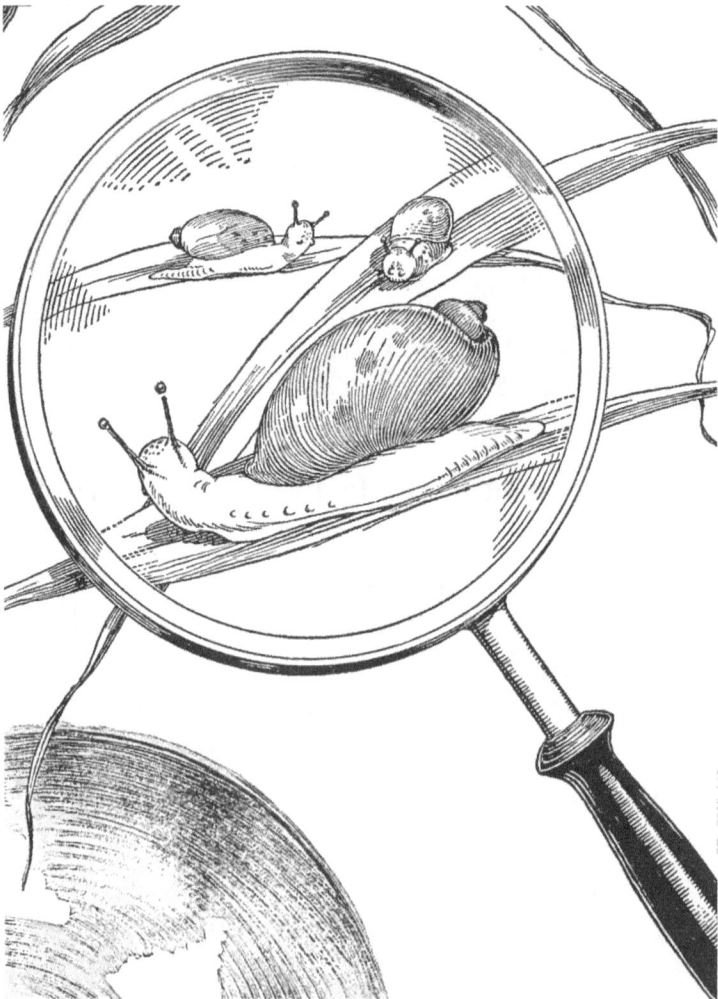

Uncle Tom gave Don and Nan a reading glass to help them see the snails.

He said, "A reading glass is not flat. It is thicker in the middle than around the edge. Some people use one to read small letters in a book."

They looked at the grown snail and the young snails through the reading glass.

Each snail had one flat foot. It put its foot out of its shell to creep. The foot was soft and wet. The snail could creep up the side of the glass.

It had four feelers in front. They looked like tiny soft horns. Two were longer than the others.

Each snail had two dark eyes. They were on the ends of the longer feelers.

The snail could pull its eyes inside of its feelers. It could pull its feelers inside of its body. It could pull its body inside of its shell.

So it had a good way to hide. It could hide in its own shell.

Ladybird's Children

Ladybird laid many eggs in one day. She put them close together on a rose leaf.

The eggs were tiny and yellow and they stood on one end.

When the baby beetles hatched they did not look like Ladybird.

They had no thin wings to fly with. They had no pretty red wing covers.

Each baby beetle had six legs to run with. When it was hungry it ran to find aphids to eat.

The young beetles were so hungry that they ate aphids for about three weeks.

Then there were not many aphids left on the rose bush.

Mr. Gray was glad when he came to look at the bush. He showed the baby beetles to Don and Nan.

He said, "Ladybird and her children are taking care of this bush.

"Young and grown Ladybirds take care of many bushes and other plants. They eat many kinds of aphids."

When the young beetles were about three weeks old, they took a rest. While they rested, their wings and wing-covers grew on their backs.

Their bodies changed in other ways while they rested. When they woke they looked like Ladybird.

Nan said, "I hope they will stay in our house next winter. Then in the spring I can watch the pretty Ladybirds fly away to a bush."

Johnny Darter

The water ran very fast in the brook. It ran over little stones.

The brook was fresh and clean. It was a good home for some water plants and some water animals.

Johnny Darter was a water animal and he lived in the brook.

He was a fish and he liked to swim in fast water.

He could swim up the brook and down the brook.

When he swam up he went head first. But when he swam down he went tail first.

Johnny Darter was a grown fish but he was a small one. He was not three inches long.

His eyes were near the top of his head. His mouth was wide. His head looked somewhat like the head of a frog. He had a row of dark marks on each side of his body.

This little fish had eight fins.

Two fins were along the middle of his back. He could put them up like little sails. Or he could put them down.

One fin was on the end of his tail.

One fin was on the middle of the under part of his body. It was not far from his tail.

Four fins were on his sides near his head. They were low on his body. There were two on each side.

He could move his four side fins like wings when he swam. He could put the ends down on the stones in the brook and walk with his fins.

One day Don and Nan caught Johnny Darter. They put him into a pail and looked at all his fins.

Then Nan said, "He is so scared! He wishes he were in the brook." So they let Johnny Darter go back to his home in the brook.

"He swims up the brook faster than the water goes down!" said Don.

A Spider's Tower

The spider's name was Wolf Spider. She had eight legs like other spiders. But her home was not like the homes of other kinds of spiders. And she had different habits.

There were some silk glands in Wolf Spider's body. Silk came out of these glands when she needed it. She did not make a web with it.

Wolf Spider dug a hole in the ground for her home. It was about ten inches long. She put silk on the inside of her hole. It was easy for her to run on the silk when she went up or down.

Wolf Spider made a tower around the top of her hole. She found some little sticks to make it with. They were one or two inches long.

She laid the sticks so that her tower had five sides. She used silk to hold each stick in the right place. She made the tower more than two inches high.

Wolf Spider often climbed her tower and watched from the top.

If she saw an insect on the ground she could jump and catch it. She liked insects to eat.

If some animal came and scared her she could hide in her hole.

So her tower was a watch tower.

One day Wolf Spider laid her eggs. There were a great many of them.

She made a silk bag for a nest. She put all her eggs in the bag.

When Wolf Spider went to any place she took her egg bag with her. She held it under her hind legs.

Some days were cold and wet. Then Wolf Spider kept her eggs at home.

On pleasant days she often took her egg bag into the sunshine. The warm sun helped the young spiders to hatch.

After a while the baby spiders were old enough to come out of the silk bag. Then their mother helped them open the bag so they could get out of it.

The baby spiders ran to their mother. They climbed to her back and other parts of her body.

Wolf Spider kept her babies with her while they were very young. She gave them rides everywhere she went.

They stayed on her back when she went hunting for food. And they had a fast ride to their safe home when she ran into the tower.

Don found the little tower one day and told Nan to come to see it.

They sat on the ground and were very quiet. At last Wolf Spider came to the top of the tower where they could watch her.

Wolf Spider watched them, too.

The Bee That Cut Leaves

Mrs. Leaf Cutter was as busy as a bumblebee or a honey bee. But she did not do the same kind of work that those other bees did. She had her own different habits.

First this little bee found a big piece of wood. It was so old that it was soft.

Next she dug a hole in the wood with her jaws.

Her jaws were like tools that she could use in many different ways. They were strong enough to dig in wood if it was soft.

When her hole was five or six inches long she flew away.

She went as far as a rose bush. Then she used her jaws again. This time she used them like little shears. They were sharp and she cut a piece out of a rose leaf. She could cut very, very quickly.

Mrs. Leaf Gutter needed many such pieces for her nests. But she could hold only one at a time. So she took each piece to her hole as soon as she cut it.

She made a nest shaped like a thimble. She had some sticky juice in her mouth. She put some on each piece of leaf to hold it in place.

When her first nest was ready she filled it with bee bread. She made this food with pollen and nectar that she got from flowers.

She drank the nectar and put the pollen on the hairs on the under part of her body. Then she took them to the nest and made bee bread.

After she filled the nest with food, she laid an egg. She put it on top of the bee bread.

Then she flew to the rose bush again. She cut a round green piece the right size to cover the nest.

Airs. Leaf Gutter made about eight rose leaf nests. They were in the hole like a row of thimbles. One was on top of another.

Each nest had one egg in it. The baby bee that hatched was soft and white. It had no legs or wings.

It ate all the bee bread that was in its own nest. That was all the food it needed. When that was gone the baby bee was not hungry.

Each baby bee changed to a pupa. It did not need to eat while it was a pupa. It rested and its body changed again.

When it had rested long enough it was not a pupa any more. It was a grown bee and looked like Mrs. Leaf Cutter.

Don and Nan saw one of these bees fly to a rose bush. She was not so large as a honey bee. She did not have so many pretty hairs as a bumblebee.

The children watched the bee cut a piece from a leaf and fly away.

"I wonder why she cut the leaf," said Nan to her brother.

Box Turtle

Box Turtle was a good name for him. He could keep his shell open or shut, somewhat like a box.

When he was scared he shut his shell and that was one way to hide.

There was a hinge in his under shell. The front end could move up to the front of his top shell. And the back end could move up to the back of his top shell. So his head and his tail and his four legs were all inside his shut shell.

The top shell was brown with yellow spots on it. The under shell was almost black and its yellow spots were bigger.

Box Turtle did not live in the water. He liked to walk on land.

When he walked, his shell was open so he could move his legs.

He put out his head and looked with his bright red eyes.

When Box Turtle was hungry he went to hunt for his food. He had many pleasant picnics.

He often caught young insects that had no wings and could not fly away. They were good meat for his dinner.

This turtle liked sweet food very much. But his head was too big to put into flowers. He could not drink nectar like a bee or a butterfly or a hummingbird.

Box Turtle had another way to get nectar. When he found some good clover blossoms he ate them. That was the way he could get the nectar that was inside the flower.

Don and Nan liked sweet food, too. When the blackberries were ripe they both went to pick some.

While they were near the bushes they saw Box Turtle. He picked berries that were near the ground. Some juice ran out of his mouth and changed the color of his face.

Nan asked, "Shall we leave all the low berries for the turtle?"

"Yes," said Don. "We will pick the berries that are too high for him to reach. We can leave the others for him. Then he can have some fun, too."

Box Turtle ate and ate and grew so fat he could not shut his shell!

Ants with Wings

Ants with wings come out of their homes in the ground. They come from many homes in different places.

All the ants of the same kind come the same day. They fly away together. There are so many ants with wings that they seem like a cloud in the air.

Soon the ants fly down to the ground and take off their wings. They do not need to use them again.

Bees and beetles and butterflies and other insects keep their wings after they are grown. They do not take them off and throw them away.

But ants have habits of their own. When their wings are grown they fly one day. The father and mother ants fly at the same time. After that they never fly again.

The mother ants tear off their own wings. Then they hunt for good places for new homes. They do not go back to their old homes.

The mother ants dig holes in new places and lay eggs. Most of the young ants grow up to be workers.

Worker ants do not have any wings. They can never fly away. They stay at home and help the mother ant. They are busy every day.

Their mother lays many, many eggs. The workers take care of the babies.

The young ants are soft and white. They have no legs. The workers take them to rooms in the ground.

Often there is a stone over one room in the home of an ant. That is a good room for baby ants.

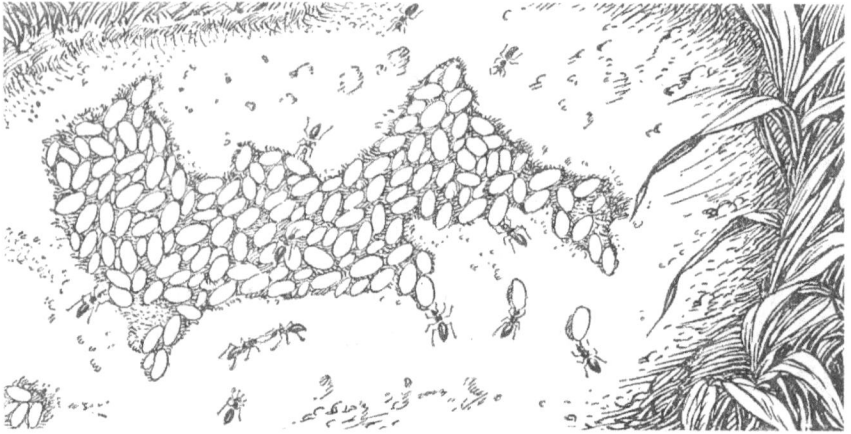

Don picked up a stone that was over some ants. He and Nan saw the white ant babies under the stone. The young ants were in cocoons. They looked like little white eggs.

The worker ants ran very fast to the cocoons. Each worker held one cocoon in her mouth and took it into another room in the ground.

Berries for Bluebirds

There were some honeysuckle bushes in the park.

Bees came to visit them in spring. They liked the nectar that they found in the pink flowers.

Soon the pink parts of the flowers fell and berries grew. There were seeds in the berries.

At first the berries were small and hard and green. When they were ripe they were soft and red.

Bluebirds visited these bushes in summer when the berries were ripe.

There were father and mother bluebirds and young bluebirds.

Some of the young birds had on their first feathers. They had little white spots on their backs. Their front feathers were brown and white. Their tails and part of the wing feathers were blue. They were too young to look like old birds.

The young birds picked berries. The old birds helped them, too. The babies opened their bills and asked for food. So the father and mother birds gave them more berries.

The bluebirds flew to other parts of the park with berries in their mouths. They dropped honeysuckle seeds in many different places.

The seeds lay on the ground all winter. In the spring they grew. So there were many little bushes in the park.

Mr. Gray showed the bushes to Don and Nan and said, "Some of these honeysuckles are too near the path. Will you help me dig them?"

Nan said, "I wish we might have all the honeysuckle bushes we dig up. We could plant them at the farm. They would grow and have pink flowers and red berries.

"Then every summer there would be more berries for bluebirds."

So Mr. Gray gave them the young bushes that were too near the path.

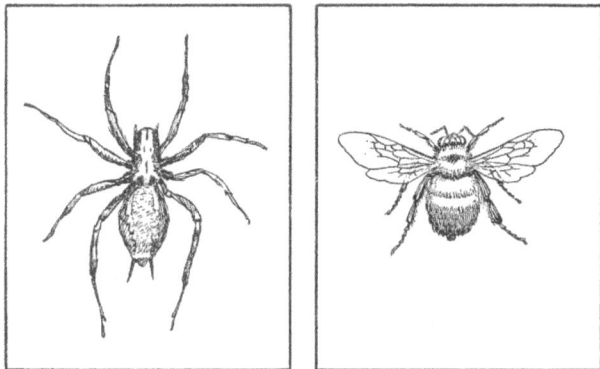

What Do You Remember?

1. Spider and Insect Pictures

Make a picture of a spider on one piece of paper.

Make a picture of a bumblebee, or some other grown insect, on another piece of paper.

Which animal will have more legs?

2. Tell About One of Them

1. In this book you have read about two kinds of spiders. Tell all you can about one of them.

2. You have read about eight, or more, kinds of insects. Tell all you can about one of them.

3. You have read about four kinds of evergreen trees. Tell all you can about one of them.

4. You have read about eight, or more, kinds of birds. Tell all you can about one of them.

5. You have read about blue flowers and yellow flowers. Tell all you can about one of them.

3. What Did They Do in Summer?

Read a line under A. Find, under B, the right line to go with it.

A

1. Mrs. Leaf Cutter
2. Father and Mother Oriole
3. The wolf spider
4. The box turtle
5. Don and Nan

B

dug a hole and made a tower.
ate some blackberries.
hunted for caterpillars.
made some leaf nests in a row.
visited plants and animals.

4. Which Word Do You Choose?

There are six lines on this page that need one more word. Choose the right word to end each line.

1. Darter is the name of a ___.

                turtle   bird   fish   insect

2. The oriole nest hangs from a ___.

              box   branch   roost   wall

3. Ladybird's little eggs were ___.

       yellow   black   white   green

4. Ladybird was a pretty little ___.

       bird   bee   fly   beetle

5. Bluebirds like honeysuckle ___.

    nectar   flowers   leaves   berries

6. Ants can take off their own ___.

    legs   wings   heads   feelers